AND YOU CAN'T
HELP BUT LISTEN

Jamie Jackman

ISBN 978-1-7782193-4-4

Text copyright © 2024 Jamie Jackman.
Series cover design by Vanessa Iddon of Perfect Day.
Design, layout, and editing by Brack and Brine.

Printed in Canada by Marquis Book Printing.
Published by Brack and Brine.

Lyrics co-written by Alicia Seaward are used with permission.
Lyrics contributed by Amelia Curran are used with permission.
Silver Wolf Band members Matthew Barrett, Justin Jackman,
and Brandon Pardy also contributed to the development of
many of these songs and have given permission for their use.

Inquiries regarding *You Can't Help But Listen* may be directed
to:

Brack and Brine
PO Box 1713 Stn B
Happy Valley-Goose Bay, NL
A0P 1E0 Canada

www.brackandbrine.com

Library and Archives Canada Cataloguing in Publication

Title: And you can't help but listen / Jamie Jackman.
Other titles: And you cannot help but listen
Names: Jackman, Jamie, author.
Description: Includes an index.
Identifiers: Canadiana (print) 20240343247 | Canadiana
(ebook) 20240344510 | ISBN 9781778219344 (softcover) | ISBN
9781778219351 (ePUB)
Subjects: LCSH: Songs, English—Canada—Texts. |
LCSH: Folk-rock music—Newfoundland and Labrador—Texts.
Classification: LCC ML54.6 .J125 2024 |
DDC 782.42166026/8—dc23

Contents

Foreword

I was first inspired to introduce myself to Jamie Jackman when I heard his song "Estuary" on the radio. This sort of thing happens among songwriters— "I heard you, you spoke to me, let's be friends..." I recognized in Jamie a sort of creative kinship. *Behold, a writer! Poor sod,* I thought. *I know a lifer when I see one.*

In the years since then, Jamie and I have shared a lot about our common love of songcraft. We joined our efforts in studio on Silver Wolf Band's *There's No Time,* which was, stop-and-start, a year-long effort. I got to start every session day with looking a fellow writer in the eye and asking, "What's this one about?" And each time, I actually got an answer. This may not seem like much, but from a song perspective, understanding the piece can be a tricky business. Unless you're Jamie Jackman.

"Write what you know" is an incomplete, over-simplified adage. A lyricist like Jamie looks deeper than that, into identity. Into landscapes and moments passed or imagined. A fraction of a second of sunlight at an angle, just so; a moment in darkness; an imprint of dust. A writer like Jamie "cannot help but listen" to these things—I like to think that's what he means.

Not a lot of songwriters stray from the bars and measures and commit things to the page. I'm chuffed for myself that I saw this coming and got to watch Jamie transform his living lyrics into equally compelling poetry. My hope for all who read this book is as it unfolded for me as well; that you cannot help but listen.

Amelia Curran

I was 10 years old and my sister drove while a Tragically Hip tape spun in the deck of our '92 Pontiac Grand Am. She explained what the songs meant to her, and that meant everything to me. She is the reason I hold words in high regard and promise to always take care of them.

I dedicate the following work to my sister, Jolene.

Author's Preface

This all began as a personal exercise to see if I could make my lyrics read like poems and my poems read like songs. Perhaps from an underlying desire to know if the words could stand on their own, without drums, piano, bass, and backing vocals. I mentioned this in passing one day to Morgen Mills, someone I've long admired as a writer and for her dedication to Labrador literature. About a month later, I received an email asking if I would be interested in having it published through Brack and Brine. I accepted without hesitation.

Then began the process of piecing lyrics and songs together in a way that made a bit of sense. I decided to start with all of the lyrics of songs I have recorded with Silver Wolf Band in chronological order, beginning with *Jam the Blues*, released in 2010, and finishing with *There's No Time*, released in 2022. Following the lyrics is a selection of sketches, as we refer to here. They are poems for now, but may very well end up on subsequent Silver Wolf Band albums. In fact, here's a little homework for you: which one of these sketches has already been released as a Silver Wolf Band song by the time this book is in your hands?

I tend to create lyrics and poems by writing down interesting words, phrases, and sentences that are largely unrelated to one another, my criteria simply being that the words and phrases must sound good on their own and trigger some type of sentimental feeling. They float around in my mind, notes, and apps, until they eventually come together, almost like in a scrapbook. Sometimes the result sounds like a song, and other times it sounds like a poem. The meaning almost always comes later.

I hope you find something within these works that makes you feel like you're looking through an old scrapbook you'd forgotten making. I believe there is no way to connect with others unless we ourselves are willing to share. And that's what this is all about: connection.

Jam the Blues
2010

Violets and Roses

There's a puzzle in life
that I just don't get.
I tried to move the pieces,
but they still won't fit.
I tried to learn to love,
so then I learned to cry.
I know I can't change your mind,
so I won't try.

There was this girl I knew,
she smelled just like flowers,
like violets and roses,
like wine and April showers.
I never asked for rain,
so she let me dry.
I know I can't change your mind,
so I won't try.

But I wish you knew
just how much you meant to me,
and I wonder why
you'd let a good thing die.

I see you standing there,
and I find it hard to swallow.
I know my face is smiling,
but inside I feel so hollow.
There'll be no apologies
after this good-bye,
but I know if you spread your wings,
you just might fly.

But I wish you knew
just how much you meant to me,
and I wonder why
you'd let a good thing die.

Silver Wolf

I have come to set the leaves on fire.
Through the wind, I heard them sing,
the raven choir.

I drew your face about a thousand times,
took the lines from my memory,
and I watched you come alive.

Can you hear the wolves crying?
Can you see the clouds swallow up the sky?
I want you here, I want you here
Through cigarettes and smoke and sweat,
I'll watch you disappear.

Saved Her from Winter

I saved her from winter,
her hair so silver.
Lifeless and lovely,
she'll die thinking of me.
   and I will

Just a day shy away,
ignorant, I say.
No, they don't feel pain,
and they never remain.
   and I will

Life fades to real time,
begin to pantomime—
a full moon stairway
to take her life away.

Fair is just a fairy tale,
her eyes so warm and pale.
I say the monsters
walk here amongst us.
   and I will

Life fades to real time,
begin to pantomime—
a full moon stairway
to take her life away.

Jam the Blues

Nighttime falls on this lonely town,
and memories come to hunt me down.
All the things I thought I lost in the past—
finally find me, they find me at last.
So, I'll sit and I'll bask in a hollow poet's glow,
singing lines by poets that he'll never know.

He'll tell me about the hand he was dealt,
about the time she left him and just how he felt
Cheer up man, don't you look so sad—
you only sing about the women that you never had.

And the beat sounds like an old man playing spoons.
The bass got one string left slipping out of tune.
The harmonica set sail on a smoky sea.
Jam the blues, boys, one more time for me.

Lovely lady sitting in her stare.
You got me all wrong, baby, don't try to care.
No, you don't have to try and pretend.
It ain't hard to tell where we have to end,
but I'll buy you a drink for a second of your time.
I feel you got to know about this sorrow of mine—

You see, like music, she slipped into my life,
but she left me just like a serrated knife,
and through an open wound, my heart fell to the floor.
Now I play my guitar, because I can't feel anymore.

And the beat sounds like an old man playing spoons.
The bass got one string left slipping out of tune.
The harmonica set sail on a smoky sea.
Jam the blues, boys, one more time for me.

Throwing Rocks At A Falling Star

With no obstruction in my view,
with no obstruction in my view,
in my ear, all I hear is you.

With no obstruction in my view,
my memory will take me back
to us lying on the sand,
throwing rocks at an empty can.

I leaned over and I said to you:
"Think this is all I am?
Throwing rocks at an empty can?"

Maybe this is all we are,
throwing rocks at a falling star.

And uncertainly committed to
the possible, the opportunity.
I'll pick up every rock until I hit it,
and I won't forget that
I'm constantly inspired by
your gentle ways, your open eyes.

And I'll take more away from you
than I'll give you credit.
Oh, I'll take more away from you
than I'll give you credit.

But I won't forget it.

Autumn Coming On

Summer has sung its song,
I feel autumn coming on.
The days don't stay too long.
I feel something's going on.
I can tell by the way you smell
you've been doing me wrong.
Summer has sung its song,
I feel autumn coming on.

Or maybe I'm just lazy,
and maybe you're just a crutch.
Or maybe I'm just crazy,
or maybe I think too much.
How much is enough?

Or maybe I just give a little way too much.
I can't go on living without your velvet touch,
your velvet touch.

If you ever need me, if you ever come to,
You know where you can find me,
I'll be lonely waiting for you.

Summer has sung its song,
I feel autumn coming on.
The days don't stay too long.
I feel something's going on.
I can tell by the way you smell
you've been doing me wrong.
Summer has sung its song,
I feel autumn coming on.

Or maybe I'll be swinging
from a garbage chandelier,
cursing the day I met you,
but still wishing that you were here.
Or maybe I'll be kissing
a painting of your face,
made from your old lipstick
and undergarment lace.
Or maybe I'll be kissing
a lady named gasoline,
or maybe I'll be smoking
and drinking Angeline.

Summer has sung its song,
I feel autumn coming on.
The days don't stay too long.
I feel something's going on.
I can tell by the way you smell
you've been doing me wrong.
Summer has sung its song,
I feel autumn coming on.

Good Night in the City

What a good night in the city,
what a good night on the town.
What a good night in the city,
what a good night on the town.

Got Bob Marley in the background
and all my friends to make that sound,
Randy Beefheart with his arms around me,
what good friends that I have found.

What a good night in the city,
what a good night on the town.
What a good night in the city,
what a good night on the town.

We are the blood in the veins of this town.
These are not streets. They're sacred ground.
Where's my love? I couldn't find her,
but she looked so pretty with the city behind her.

What a good night in the city,
what a good night on the town.
What a good night in the city,
what a good night on the town.

And I cannot promise you anything,
and I cannot promise you anything today.

Pockets Filled with Rocks
2018

A Thousand Years

I used to play on the river
like moonlight on the lops,
like an Elder speaking
whose spirit never stops—
so ancient, patient,
moving like the breeze,
drinking the water
that's reflected the leaves
for a thousand years.

I used to speak to the river
in words I'd understand,
then kill my dinner
and eat it with my hands—
so endless, relentless,
so restless and free.
Respect for the water
that's been so good to me
for a thousand years.

Like the geese in the fall,
you have somewhere to be.
I'm a seal in the springtime,
caught on a floe—
I don't know where I'm going,
just happy to go.

Let me paint you a picture
of a wild land,
sewn together by the grace
of a weathered hand—
so cast off and signed off,
I'm not ready to leave,
like the fading memories
of the old man and me,
for a thousand years

I'm dreaming of the stream
and I don't want to leave,
like the fading memories
of the old man and me,
for a thousand years.

Butter And Snow

I want to live in Butter and Snow,
where I watched my mom and dad get old.
Deep in the heart of this great big bay,
they'll bury my bones someday.

Because I learned to love in Butter and Snow,
holding hands down at the shore—
I remember that sunny day
when you told me you were going away
and your folks decided that they'd split for town.
I decided that I'd stick around,
but I don't regret it a day.

This is my home; this is where I belong,
and if you don't like it, the rabbits won't mind,
and if you can't wait, baby, all I have is time,
but no mind to convince you to stay—
My words are few, but my heart finds a way.

Because I want to live in Butter and Snow,
where I watched my mom and dad get old
Deep in the heart of this great big bay,
They'll bury my bones some day.

But you won't have to dig deep to find me—

Oh, my soul will be in a cabin
down Butter and Snow,
Falling asleep beneath the stars.
Falling asleep beneath the stars,
oh, my soul!

Autumn Wandering

I'm gonna find a peaceful nature
where the wind comes from.
I'm gonna find a peaceful nature
when I'm done.

Where questions are answered,
and your wounds disappear—
I'm gonna find a peaceful nature,
just not here, just not here.

But I'll get a world away.
I won't send you letters—I'll pray,
and I'd give my world
to get a world away.

How pretty you must've looked
in the bonfire glow.
I remember how you wrote our names
with ashes in the snow.

I'll come out here, way out here,
and let this song just write itself,
listening to the fire crackling,
put another book on my shelf.

Because questions are answered,
and your wounds disappear—
I'm gonna find a peaceful nature.
It's right here, it's right here.

I'll get a world a way.
I won't send you letters—I'll pray,
and I'd give my world
to get a world away.

North Atlantic April

"Daddy, I love the wind," she said,
with tears in her eyes and her cheeks turning red
and her pockets filled with rocks,
bottle caps, and dandelion tops.

Like a North Atlantic April,
you're so young and you're so capable.
Like a North Atlantic April,
you're golden, unmistakable,
but you're as cold and you're as distant
as the shores of Labrador.

Little hands as cold as ice—
the sun sits low, like it's afraid of heights.
Little feet that won't hesitate—
you've got time, but not enough to wait.

Like a North Atlantic April,
you're so young and you're so capable.
Like a North Atlantic April,
you're golden, unmistakable,
but you're as cold and you're as distant
as the shores of Labrador.

Little hands as cold as ice—
the sun sits low, like it's afraid of heights.
There's still some winter to this wind—
"Hold me now, Daddy, I don't wanna go in."

I'm mountain to this rock,
I'm a puddle to the lake,
too serious to laugh,
too sacred to mistake.

Like a North Atlantic April,
you're so young and you're so capable.

Canoe

This water is too muddy to see through.
I fell out of a canoe.
I couldn't swim, and somehow you knew.

We sat and threw rocks at the water all day.
I held onto the words you said.
I was a lie, and you spoke the truth.

Strong words are easy to say,
but they're harder than blood to wash away.
There is nothing easy about this.

The night came on with its threatening chill.
The wind died down and the water got still.
You said, "I can't believe it's August!"

"I could talk to the water all day.
It carries my thoughts away."
That's totally something you'd say.

Strong words are easy to say,
but they're harder than blood to wash away.
There is nothing easy about this.

You held my hand under freezing water.
You broke my heart and ruined the summer.

You held my hand under freezing water.
You broke my heart and ruined the summer.

Strong words are easy to say,
but they're harder than blood to wash away.
There is nothing easy about this,
at all.

I moved through ages trying to get over you.
They say it goes away in time,
but I don't think that's true.

Sometimes we get left behind,
and there's simply nothing left to find.

October Already

October already,
and it already feels
like we've been here forever.
Cold breaks the deal
as we head into this dull refrain.
Take comfort in change.

Oh, the comfort we feel
as the world lays down
with its promise to keep,
that all life must end.
The poet comes alive
as the world falls to sleep.

The wind doesn't take a breath,
blowing hard against the lines.
Things never fall in place,
but they fall out sometimes.
Take comfort in change.

Oh, the comfort we feel
as the world lays down
with its promise to keep
that all life must end.
The poet comes alive
as the world falls to sleep.
I feel I'm heading home.

All life is letting go—
         of what you think you know
no choice but to turn—
         my face to the snow
no choice but to take—
         comfort in change
take comfort in change.

Summer Wind

Never thought I'd settle for bad timing,
but I've been in the wrong place too many times.
Always said that I wouldn't go down easy,
but pride goes down smooth with a bottle of wine.

There we were, just headed for the highway.
Somehow, we knew we'd be home before our time.
What I wouldn't give to be on that highway,
driving with you just one more time.

Summer wind, where did you go to?
Are you scared?
Are you lost in the places you begin?
Can I catch up to you?
Can you make me feel brand new,
if I promise I can help
with all the things that are asked of you?

Sandy girl with rainbows up in her hair—
Felt so close, but I fell so far behind.
I often wonder where she's to,
and how she's doing,
and if I ever even cross her mind.
And if I ever even cross her mind.

Summer wind, where did you go to?
Are you scared?
Are you lost in the places you begin?
Can I catch up to you?
Can you make me feel brand new,
if I promise I can help
with all the things that are asked of you?

Trap Cove Lullaby

co-written by Alicia Seaward

I want to sail away with you
through the wind out on the ocean,
a salty rainbow spraying over me,

and those islands in the distance
seem to catch the sunset falling,
each one with a story of its own.

And the one that I recall,
where the wind wouldn't let you fall—
with you there beside me,
I wasn't scared at all.

With your blue eyes on the skies,
and my green eyes on the ocean,
I could hear the harbour sing to me

in a voice so full of wisdom,
in an ancient melody,
singing, "By the time
I get to Trap Cove, I'll be free."

And the song I sang for you
about the hills where the berries grew,
when I close my eyes,
I can still see you waltzing to.

I want to sail away with you
through the wind out on the ocean,
a salty rainbow spraying over me.

Storms and Prayers
2020

Estuary

Don't you forget
that you were born before the storm
came crashing through the thickets.

Don't you forget
that you were born before the rain
started coming down in buckets.

You were fifty pounds soaking wet,
but I could see you from a mile away,
so cold and hard,
but more like ice than granite,
a distant star,
or more of a moon than a planet—
estuary, estuary.

Make no mistake,
you'll make no mistake
you weren't meant to make.
And there's no such thing,
there's no such thing
as "no such thing."

And I know,
I know, or so I'm told,
and so it goes, you'll bear no load
you weren't meant to carry.

You were fifty pounds soaking wet,
but I could see you from a mile away,
so cold and hard, but more like ice than granite,
a distant star, or more of a moon than a planet—
estuary, estuary.

This is not a bay, no, this is an estuary.
You said, "It's not a bay, no, no, no, no,
it's more of an estuary."

You are not a bay,
you are an estuary,
estuary, estuary.

Until You Come Home

a new verse for "Sons of Labrador," by Sid Dicker

I left my heart on a mountain
that overlooks a snowy valley
where the wind that swept
seemed to say,

"I'll miss you more than ever,
but I'll keep your heart right here
until you come home."

Storms

If I don't see you in my dreams tonight,
I'll see you in the morning
with a cup of tea and the radio
telling sailors to take warning.

But storms will pass before my love,
and with a little help from God above,
you'll still be holding my hand—
Be my woman, and I'll be your man.

If I don't see you in my dreams tonight,
I'll see you in the morning.
If the weather is holding off,
or the weather is holding close,
Whatever the weather, we'll stick together,
button your sweater, and let's go.

Because storms will pass before my love,
and with a little help from God above,
you'll still be holding my hand—
Be my woman, and I'll be your man.

Why do I do this to myself?

You've got a windy heart, and you know it's true
that as you fall apart, I can't help but feel for you.
But you can't steal the moon from the sky,
and you can't borrow a heart.

But storms will pass before my love,
and with a little help from God above,
you'll still be holding my hand—
You'll tell me your worries and I'll understand.

Why do you do this to yourself?

Because storms will pass before my love,
and with a little help from God above,
you'll still be holding my hand—
Be my woman, and I'll be your man.

Why do we do this to ourselves?

If I don't see you in my dreams tonight,
I'll see you in the morning.

Prayers

Winter is holding my breath,
springtime is breathing out,
and the summer is just the answer
to the prayers we said in the autumn—
prayers unspoken, forgotten.

Back in the summer when I learned to drown—
because you were never around—
I kept on thrashing until I made no sound.
I don't remember jumping in,
but I remember sinking.

And if the winter is holding my breath,
springtime is breathing out,
and the summer is just the answer
to the prayers we said in the autumn—
prayers unspoken, forgotten.

I paddled your deep waters,
so silent and so still.
Oh, how I miss your harborous heart,
and oh, my darling, I think that I always will.

And if the winter is holding my breath,
springtime is breathing out,
and the summer is just the answer
to the prayers we said in the autumn—
prayers unspoken, forgotten.

Long Way Home

She said to me, she said,
I heard that God is dead.
It was in a book I read
somewhere, sometime ago.

Thought I'd rejoice and sing.
I thought I'd fly on an angel's wing.
I thought I'd stand to greet my king
and bow.

But all I know is it's a long way home,
if you turn back now.
Just close your eyes and don't look down.
It's a long way home,
if you turn back now.

She came to me and cried,
said, all that I love has died.
When will this pain subside?
It's been hurting for quite some time.

If we're feathers of an eagle's wing,
then we're stones by a babbling spring,
and we're one voice when we all sing,
but I don't know how.

And all I know is it's a long way home,
if you turn back now.
Just close your eyes and don't look down.
It's a long way home,
if you turn back now.

Get Outta Here

You can't call this
anything you know,
when you're living
just for the taking
and nothing is as calming
as the freezing rain,
pouring down so miserable,
tired, and the same.

Let's get outta here.
Let's get outta here.

Darling, darling,
what do you say?
We'll leave this town tonight,
be on our way.
You say it ain't right,
though you know it's right.
We don't leave this town
without some kind of fight.

Let's get outta here.
Let's get outta here,
get, get, get, get, get outta here,
get, get, get, get, get outta here.

It's hard to feel
like summertime
when the rain won't stop
and the sun won't shine.
Take your heart off your sleeve
and stuff it in your shoes.
We both know we ain't
got any time to lose.

Let's get outta here.
Let's get outta here,
get, get, get, get, get outta here,
get, get, get, get, get outta here.

There's No Time
2022

Settling Dust

I was eight years old
at the top of my stairs
when the cops came by.
I had a tear in my eye.
My older brother said,
"Don't get sentimental on me, man."
Ah, but ever since then,
I feel like I'm settling.

Settling dust we never stirred up.
       settling dust
Settling dust we never stirred up,
throwing guts to the gulls
in the capital of character,
settling dust we never stirred up.

I'm gonna paint a picture of the sky,
call it "God Passes By."
I'll drag my brush through the paint
with the patience of a saint,
thinking over, and over, and over, and over—
Don't get sentimental on me, man.

Don't get sentimental on me, man.
Ah, but ever since then I feel like I'm settling.

Settling dust we never stirred up.
      settling dust
Settling dust we never stirred up,
throwing guts to the gulls
in the capital of character,
settling dust we never stirred up.

Eighteenth Century

The heart of the eighteenth century.
The heart of the eighteenth century,
but the world has been discovered.
There's nothing left to uncover,
but you've got
the heart of the eighteenth century.

Captain the Age of Discovery,
bestow on me my agency.
If the sea can't be my lover,
I'll lean onto my brother
for the heart of the eighteenth century.

And I will wait
on the coastline for you.
          I'll wait on the coastline.

I'll sit, and I'll listen
for your signal cutting through.
          I'll wait on the coastline.

Yes, I will wait
on the coastline for you.
          I'll wait on the coastline.

I'll sit and I'll watch
until your light comes guiding through.

Endeavour, the Terror, the Mystery.
Trial, and the error, and the misery.
The water is icy, dark and deep,
but we've got miles to go before we reach
the heart of the eighteenth century.

The heart of the eighteenth century,
but the world has been discovered.
There's nothing left to uncover,
but you've got
the heart of the eighteenth century.

And I will wait
on the coast line for you.
> *I'll wait on the coast line.*

I'll sit, and I'll listen
for your signal cutting through.
> *I'll wait on the coast line.*

Yes, I will wait
on the coast line for you.
> *I'll wait on the coast line.*

I'll sit and I'll watch
until your light comes guiding through.

Falling Asleep

I should be falling asleep.
Instead, I'm falling apart.

I'm holding hands with your memory,
alone in the dark.
When I'm at a loss for words,
I think about you,
and they come right to me.
You pick the jam and refresh the well.
I thought I heard you say something—
I couldn't tell.

See what you do to me, raven-haired beauty?
You wake up the poet asleep in my heart,
and it's not that we couldn't keep going,
it's just that we never could start.

I need a face for the name;
I need a place for the blame.
I'm not asking a lot,
short of all that you've got,
and when I could not escape myself,
you'd drop everything and run right to me,
and pick the lock to my cell.
I thought I heard you say something—
I couldn't tell.

See what you do to me, raven-haired beauty?
You wake up the poet asleep in my heart,
and it's not that we couldn't keep going,
it's just that we never could start.

See what you do to me, raven-haired beauty?
We weathered the storm together,
and to our surprise,
in our world it never stopped snowing,
and now we are buried alive—

And it won't survive.
We are buried alive.
No, we won't survive.

See what you do to me, raven-haired beauty?
You wake up the poet asleep in my heart,
and it's not that we couldn't keep going,
it's just that we never could start.

I should be falling asleep.
Instead, I'm falling apart.

Adlatok

An old house still stands
near the contentious water,
growing willows and birches,
not strong sons and daughters.

Generations strewn like seeds on a gale,
far from the old house up Adlatok
or the mission at Hopedale.

If I get back, know this is true:
I'll never be in a rush to leave you.

If I should die before I return,
bury me as deep as you can
in the rocks, the soil, the frost and the sod,
to Moravian hymns and the words of God,
so my body may mix with my ancestors' bones, and
get Harry Martin to sing, "This Is My Home."

Your Name and Where You're From

Let's skip the long introduction—
Just your name and where you are from.

Keep this to an hour or so
out of respect for everyone,
and if we stick to the agenda,
maybe get a few things done,
there'll be time enough toward the end
to exchange our information
so we can do this all again.

But can you repeat the question?
You're breaking up on me.
I didn't mean to cut you off, my friend,
or to move along so easily.

Geese and the Wind

with contributions from Amelia Curran

I woke up from the wind,
and now I can't get back to sleep again.
I am struggling with the silence of this room.

Laying motionless
and begging God to give me rest,
tormented by a hag sitting on my chest.

To the geese and the wind—
Take me with you south
where the fruit ripens
and will fall into our mouths.

I woke up from the wind,
and now I can't get back to sleep again.
I am struggling with the ghosts inside my tomb.

There are men at sea
who would probably trade places with me,
but I can't get perspective now.

So, to the geese and the wind—
Take me with you south
where the fruit ripens
and will fall into our mouths.

Run away, run away, like there's no time.
      Run away, run away.
Run away, run away, like there's no time.
Run away, there's no time.
There's no time.

To the geese and the wind—
Take me with you south
where the fruit ripens
and will fall into our mouths.

Responsible

I live in a bay where I was born,
but never really meant to stay.
Sure, I'll complain, but I'll do it in a subtle way,
like when I'm sad and I miss you,
but I don't know how to tell you
without making you feel responsible,
without making you feel responsible.

Lie in my bed just trying,
trying to cover all my tracks,
but I don't know how to say,
"I can't hear you, and I don't know where I'm at,"
without making you feel responsible,
without making you feel responsible

You hold in your hands
all the things of mine,
things you cannot borrow—
but it's not that you can't have it.
No, it's that you can't give it back
without making yourself responsible,
without making yourself responsible.

Over, Under, and Around

You'd never say tomorrow is December,
if it wasn't for the chill I feel in the air,
but you go on blaming it on the weather,
though we both know there's no snow out there.

I still believe there's a way
over and under and around
everything in front of me.

The frost in the night knits a sweater
all across my window pane,
and the moon shines on forever,
as if forever was just another day.

I still believe there's a way
over and under and around
everything in front of me.

You're a stone skipping on calm water
to a beat that's pumping like a heart.
I don't know where this ends, my love—
I'm waiting on you to show me where to start.

Because I still believe there's a way
over and under and around
everything in front of me.

Sketches

Stories

You're much too late, my son.
Everyone has come and gone.
You can talk to the rocks,
but they don't really listen.

Keeping company with ghosts,
stubborn as a dog at post,
they sing ancient songs by night,
and you can't help but listen.

My cabin walls are bent and old,
like stories that've long been told,
worn 'neath weary windows,
tired floors awake with sound.

Imagination, cast your hook
from the shores of a dog-eared book
while embers pulse an amber light
and snicker like a friend of mine.

Every Bone In My Heart

You were the brightest star
on the darkest night of my life,
like a lighthouse burning
at the edge of my mind.

You tilled the fallow fields
in the acreage of my dreams.
You were an auger turning.
I was the grassy weeds.

Drop by drop, our love became a lake,
and lake by lake, the sea—
explored our constellations
until we mapped the galaxy.

Then one day I fell from your sky
and broke every bone in my heart.

Butterflies in a Clover Field

I was catching butterflies
in a clover field
under endless, deep blue skies,
my favourite memory
reflected in
the black of her green eyes.

Purple flowers shook their heads
in joyful adulation
of all the things
love's season brings,
like fluttering hearts
and delicate wings
and birds on perches
adorning the birches,
offering blessing
under blue skies undressing.

Oh! To be catching butterflies
in a clover field
the third week of July,
and let summer's breath,
fill our chests
as the days trip slowly by.

All I Love Has Gone Away

I watched the sun set in the morning.
I watched the flowers die in May.
Unnatural and without warning,
all I love has gone away.

I wear my sorrow like a sweater
against the softening light of day.
Still the winter wind keeps whispering,
"All I love has gone away."

Evening creeps through my curtain,
waltzes me across the floor,
unwavering but still uncertain.
All I loved walked out the door.

I wish my memory would forget me,
but it knows every hiding place.
Now I cling to cliffs of misery,
for all I love has gone away.

Throwaway Thoughts

You said you dreamed of me,
said I dreamed of you
and that you were smitten,
when I used the word "smitten."

Can't tell you what I want,
but I'm always here to listen,
and you know,
like the weather man knows—
if it's minus twenty,
it's too cold to snow.

But I'm thankful for the night,
we got in a fight,
and you know,
I wouldn't be surprised
if you told me to my face,
everything is about to change.

It's hard, and it's scary.
If you're loved, you're lucky.
Being loved is a luxury.
I just wish this me
wouldn't die in his sleep.

Warm March Morning

On a warm March morning,
I awake to the sound
of wind off the ice in the harbour,
just steps away from my cabin door.

Staring out the window
like mother would always do,
I see ptarmigan tracks
in the snow, fresh and new.

I watch the wind tip the willows
in my direction for a while,
then pile some wood
in my father's old woodstove,
then brandish some matches
and get ready to vanquish
that old evening dampness.

Old Soul (Guitar)

You're an old soul,
just like my favourite guitar,
with scars on your body
and scars on your heart,
like the taste of Irish whiskey
or the smell of cigarettes.

You carry heavy memories
and names I'd rather forget,
and every time I pick you up,
it gets harder to put you down.

Sometimes you're a funeral—
other times you sound
like a night on the town.

Old Soul (North Star)

Did you ever think it would come to this?
Blowing the driveway, blowing a kiss,
measuring the days in lightyears,
drying the dishes, drying your tears.

You're an old soul,
just like the North Star.
I don't know where I am,
until I know where you are.

I was counting my blessings,
you were counting by twos.
I was tying up loose ends,
you were tying your shoes,
playing hide-and-go-seek,
imaginary friends,
making up stories,
making your bed.

You're an old soul,
just like the North Star.
I don't know where I am,
until I know where you are.

For however long forever is,
I hope you always remember this:
Goodnight Moon and goodnight songs,
dancing barefoot out on the lawn,
how a borrowing sun is never too shy
to beg forgiveness of a merciful sky.
That's all there is—I have no more notes
for a girl named after a song I wrote.

You're an old soul,
just like the North Star.
I don't know where I am,
until I know where you are.

Violet Rose

In the night, in the night,
sleeping as she grows,
somewhere far from the lights of town
sleeps my Violet Rose.

I'm so lucky to be the one she chose.
God bless the light that shines
on my Violet Rose.

In the night, in the night,
sleeping as she dreams,
somewhere far from my arms
sleeps a girl who means—

Everything! Everything!
Everything, you see!

God bless the day that brings
my Violet back to me.

William James

William James, William James,
tell them that's what your name is.

The farmer and the fisherman,
the hunter and the gatherer.
A hundred years, a hundred more
to tell them of them of the men
who came before you—

William James, William James,
tell them that's what your name is!

I

It snowed the day you left.
I prayed for a weather delay.
Must've been an opening
that helped you get away.

II

She's Northern light,
she's alpenglow,
pretty as new fallen snow.

III

As tales grow tall like paper birches
standing around abandoned churches,
long like shadows quick forgotten
or buried secrets, deep and rotten,
words, like wounds, crack, scar and heal,
and the only thing you know is real
is how you feel.
So, how do you feel?

IV

The summer with her fall-coloured hair
trips toward me head-first,
with a fleck of springtime in her eyes
and the winter in her fists.

V

Corvid bird perched atop
the stand of burned-out birches,
above the oily ashen earth
and smoky blackberry bushes.

VI

While collecting my heart
along the willowed shore,
left there in pieces
by those I'd loved before,

I noticed the edges
weren't sharp or precious,
but rugged and smooth,
like glass on the beaches
of oceans and bays
and far-flung reaches.

VII

No one knows how much time we have left.
I just know it isn't enough.

VIII

Let my arms be your harbour,
let my hands be your sail,
far from the wind,
high above the gale.

IX

Headlights and sleepy eyes,
frosty fallen trees
so pretty in the sunrise,
an ineffability.

X

My flower, don't turn your back on the sun.
We're all chipping at a mountain
that's growing by the tonne.

XI

I was down by the river,
deep in the willows,
lost in my thoughts,
being eaten by mosquitos.

Then I got to skipping rocks
as if it were my business,
trampling the dandelions,
wasting all the wishes.

XII

I used to test the water
when I was an amateur.
Now I am an animal,
now I am a natural.

XIII

Sleepy, subarctic winter sun,
smudges across a naked sky,
careful and slow, afraid of heights,
spending her light on waning days,
but giving not her warmth away.

Dutiful somnambulant jewel,
a captive of dusky black spruce,
subdued by cold, wintry hues,
and incandescent silhouettes,
flattering light before she sets.

XIV

August, be good to me.
Fill my nights with love and wine
and my long days with poetry.
Don't act like you didn't know that we
weren't headed for catastrophe.

All this is new to me.
It takes time to draw a line,
exalting all my memories.
Don't act like you didn't know that we
weren't reading from our eulogy.

XV

Where the sun rises from the beach
until it falls into a lake,
where the quiet of the evening
left the dreamers wide awake,
where the wind blows through windrows,
through the willows and the sand,
where my time froze just like water
until it melted through my hands.

XVI

I'll just take a minute
to sit right down in it,
the sorrow I feel for your loss.
It's the least I could do
when you're feeling blue,
wandering alone with your thoughts.

Happy it's Christmas,
just wish you were with us
to share with us all of your love.
Takes me a minute
to rid myself of it—
old feelings hang on like the frost.

XVII

You're not Cinderella,
you're not even close.
You're more like Pinocchio,
with a broken nose.

XVIII

I've been in no rush to get home
Up and down frozen town roads,
Christmas sweater, Halloween clothes,
broken hearted and bloody nosed.

I can always keep going.
Even if it starts snowing,
I'll light my way knowing
your heart stopped glowing—

I can scavenge the pieces
of broken-down and second-hand hearts.
I'll turn the engines hoping
For something to start.

XIX

Good night, my little light.
You shine as bright as the day.
I wouldn't change a thing about you.
Wish I could keep you this way.

XX

Does winter worry about me?
Two ambiguous points of time,
something there in between—
Moving goal posts, drifting lines.

I too can be deep and enduring,
set deadlines like snares,
then wander aimless, sleepy,
cold and unaware.

We bottle seasonal bounties,
carry water, cut the wood.
Does winter worry about me?
Probably not,
but it should.

XXI

I brought you coffee in the morning
like a job I had to do.
You were listening for me,
but you'd always act surprised.
Every time, but that's so you,
selflessly self-assured.

I watched the sun
set into the unsettling.
You watched me
as light left your eyes,
left your heart,
left your lungs.

I'm still pulled by the moon,
warmed by the sun.
What does the winter want me to do?
I wasn't ready to do this without you.

Index

Song Titles

First Lines

Acknowledgements

Thank you to Brack and Brine for taking this on and handling it with such care and professionalism. To Amelia for being such an inspiration and a mentor to me in so many ways. It means the world that you would take time to write a foreword for me for this book. Most importantly my parents, Bob and Irene. I still vividly recall my Dad standing in a three-quarters empty bar in Charlottetown, PEI, at 1:00 am to catch our set at Baba's Lounge, beaming with pride. It's your kind of support that kept Silver Wolf Band going when we still had so much further to go. To my bandmates: Justin, my brother who is more like my best friend, and Matthew and Bon, my best friends who are more like brothers: thank you guys for trusting me to write the songs to which you have dedicated so much of your talent and precious time. Violet and William, I hope that someday this small book makes you feel proud and inspires you to follow your dreams no matter what. You have been my inspiration through the most beautiful days and the wickedest storms. To Mckenzie, my Northern light, I am so happy to be on this journey through life together with you. Your loving pushes in the right direction and unwavering belief in everything I do continue to illuminate paths I didn't know were ever there—a little late, but right on time.

Nothing I do is without a tremendous amount of encouragement and support from those closest to me, and I cannot thank you all enough. I'll always take more away from you than I can ever give you credit. Just know that continuing to write is my futile attempt to do just that.

About the Author

Jamie Jackman is a founding member and lyricist of the multi-award-winning folk-rock group Silver Wolf Band. Born and mostly raised in Happy Valley-Goose Bay, he is of mixed Inuit and settler descent, with strong family ties to the community of Hopedale, Nunatsiavut. He is a father to Violet and William and lives in Happy Valley-Goose Bay with his partner, Mckenzie.

Brack and Brine publishes beautiful books that matter to the North. Previous titles include:

Labrador, a Reader's Guide
by Robin McGrath

and

Labrador Cinema
by Mark David Turner and Morgen Mills